My Little Notebook

2021

12

Monday	Tuesday	Wednesday
		01
06	07	08
13	14	15
20	21	22
27	28	29

Thursday	Friday	Saturday	Sunday
02	03	04	05
09	10	11	12
16	17	18	19
23	24	25	26
30	31		

Monday	Tuesday	Wednesday
03	04	05
10	11	12
17	18	19
24	25	26
31		

2022

01

@chinyun_18

Thursday	Friday	Saturday	Sunday
		01	02
06	07	08	09
13	14	15	16
20	21	22	23
27	28	29	30

2022

Monday	Tuesday	Wednesday
	01	02
07	08	09
14	15	16
21	22	23
28		

Thursday	Friday	Saturday	Sunday
03	04	05	06
10	11	12	13
17	18	19	20
24	25	26	27

2022

03

Monday	Tuesday	Wednesday
	01	02
07	08	09
14	15	16
21	22	23
28	29	30

Thursday	Friday	Saturday	Sunday
03	04	05	06
10	11	12	13
17	18	19	20
24	25	26	27
31			

2022

04

| 04 | 05 | 06 |

| 11 | 12 | 13 |

| 18 | 19 | 20 |

| 25 | 26 | 27 |

Thursday	Friday	Saturday	Sunday
	01	02	03
07	08	09	10
14	15	16	17
21	22	23	24
28	29	30	

2022

05

Monday	Tuesday	Wednesday
02	03	04
09	10	11
16	17	18
23	24	25
30	31	

Thursday	Friday	Saturday	Sunday
			01
05	06	07	08
12	13	14	15
19	20	21	22
26	27	28	29

2022

08

06	07	08
13	14	15
20	21	22
27	28	29

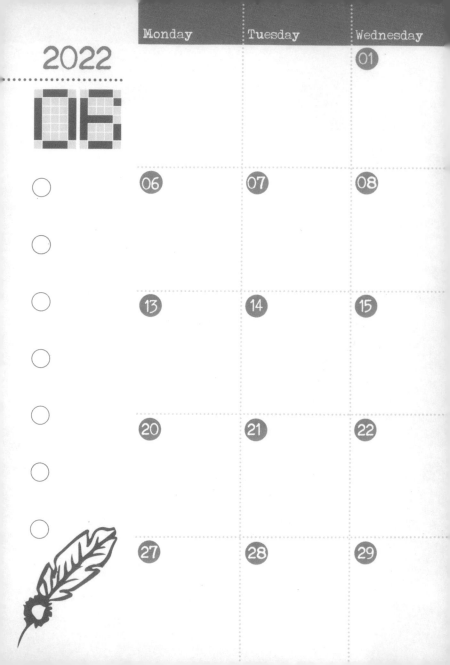

Thursday	Friday	Saturday	Sunday
02	03	04	05
09	10	11	12
16	17	18	19
23	24	25	26
30			

2022

Monday	Tuesday	Wednesday
04	05	06
11	12	13
18	19	20
25	26	27

Thursday	Friday	Saturday	Sunday
	01	02	03
07	08	09	10
14	15	16	17
21	22	23	24
28	29	30	31

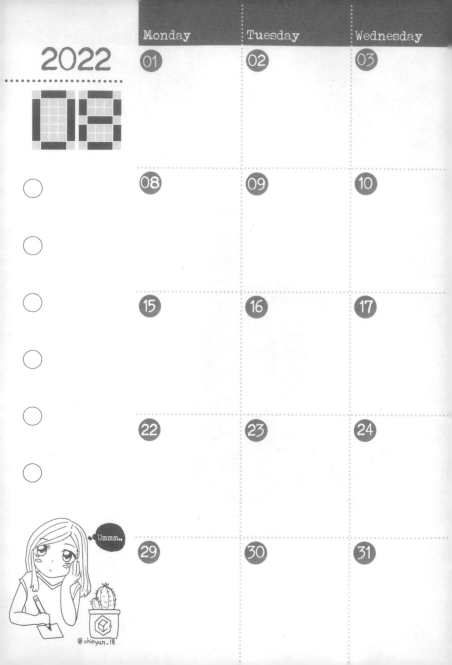

Thursday	Friday	Saturday	Sunday
04	05	06	07
11	12	13	14
18	19	20	21
25	26	27	28

2022

03

05　06　07

12　13　14

19　20　21

26　27　28

Thursday	Friday	Saturday	Sunday
01	02	03	04
08	09	10	11
15	16	17	18
22	23	24	25
29	30		

2022

10

Monday	Tuesday	Wednesday
03	04	05
10	11	12
17	18	19
24	25	26
31		

Thursday	Friday	Saturday	Sunday
		01	02
06	07	08	09
13	14	15	16
20	21	22	23
27	28	29	30

2022

11

Monday	Tuesday	Wednesday
	01	02
07	08	09
14	15	16
21	22	23
28	29	30

Thursday	Friday	Saturday	Sunday
03	04	05	06
10	11	12	13
17	18	19	20
24	25	26	27

2022

12

○ 　05　06　07

○

○ 　12　13　14

○

○ 　19　20　21

○

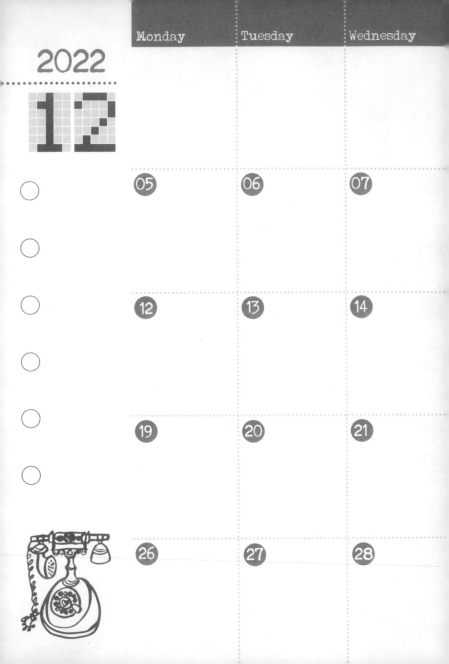

26　27　28

Thursday	Friday	Saturday	Sunday
01	02	03	04
08	09	10	11
15	16	17	18
22	23	24	25
29	30	31	

2023

01

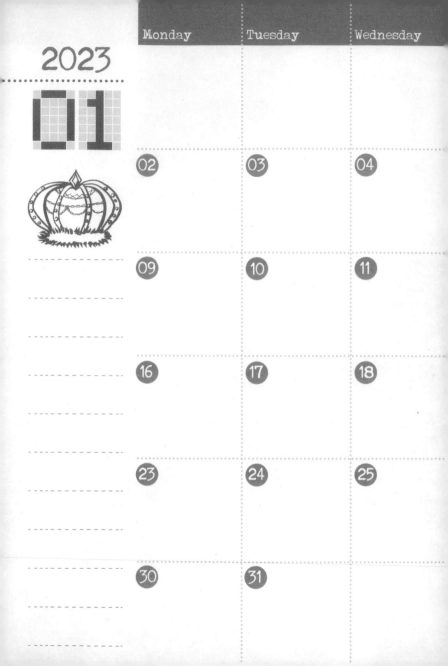

Monday	Tuesday	Wednesday
02	03	04
09	10	11
16	17	18
23	24	25
30	31	

Thursday	Friday	Saturday	Sunday
			01
05	06	07	08
12	13	14	15
19	20	21	22
26	27	28	29

2023

	Monday	Tuesday	Wednesday
			01
○	06	07	08
○			
○	13	14	15
○			
○	20	21	22
○			
	27	28	

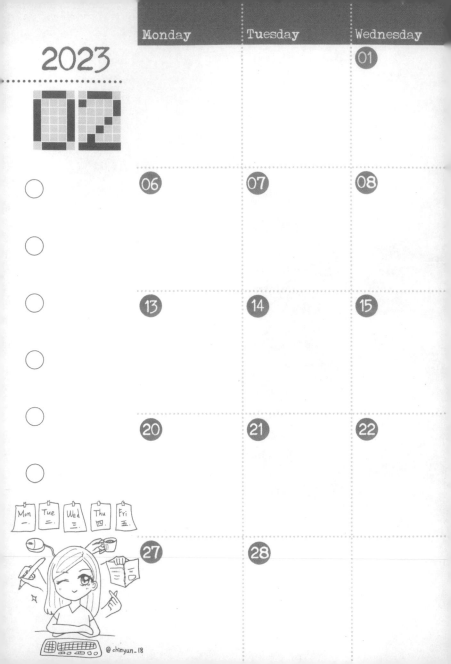

@ chinyun_18

Thursday	Friday	Saturday	Sunday
02	03	04	05
09	10	11	12
16	17	18	19
23	24	25	26

幸好我愛笑！笑一笑自己～

生活，也就沒那麼糟糕！

如果身前有陰影，
回頭～
那是因為陽光在你身後。

希望！
一顆種子可以
　　變成一片原野！

讓我們擁有，
長在心底的善良，
刻在骨子裏的堅強。

珍惜，
不要等到來不及。

用愛生活，就有幸福。

用愛工作，可以遇見更好的自己。

人生有三樣東西無法挽留～
生命・時間・愛

每個人身上都有太陽，
要懂得讓它發光！

有怒的人告訴你～
他很強大。
有愛的人告訴你～
你很強大。

如果因他人的聲音起伏
而左右了我的前進，

那就永遠也不能～
好好做自己了……

生活豈能百般如意
有一些遺憾．
我們才會～有所追尋．

不可能讓～
所有人都喜歡你，
就讓自己～
平常心待人接物。

My Little Notebook

作　　　者	林志玲 CHILING LIN
發　行　人	財團法人臺北市志玲姊姊慈善基金會
執　行　長	ANNE HSIAO
創意設計主編	SUNNY CHEN
插　　　畫	北埔國小舞蹈隊 – 沁筠、辰宣
地　　　址	106 台北市大安區羅斯福路二段 105 號 5 樓之一
電　　　話	+886-2-2366-0793
郵　　　箱	chilingjj@chilingjj.org
官　　　網	www.chilingjj.org
出　版　社	商周出版
印　　　刷	秋雨創新股份有限公司
版　　　次	2021 年 11 月 01 日　Printed in Taiwan
版 權 聲 明	版權所有 ◆ 翻印必究

瞭解志玲姊姊基金會
To understand us

聯繫志玲姊姊基金會
To contact us

支持志玲姊姊基金會
To support us